MW01519694

AMAZING Love

AMAZING *Love*

NIKKI SPEER

Pleasant Word
A Division of WINEPRESS PUBLISHING

Pleasant Word (a division of WinePress Publishing, PO Box 428, Enumclaw, WA 98022) functions only as book publisher. As such, the ultimate design, content, editorial accuracy, and views expressed or implied in this work are those of the author.

ISBN 1-4141-0572-X
Library of Congress Catalog Card Number: 2005907964

Dedication

To my wonderful,
supportive husband and my sweet boy

Table of Contents

Preface

To the unique, young women who are about to read this book, you are my motivation and the reason why God wants me to write. My crisis pregnancy became God's opportunity. God chose to show me how real He is, what love is, how to live daily for Him and march on with my head held high.

No matter what the sin, God is faithful; he will forgive and restore. Let's stop the crisis pregnancy epidemic by finding out who we are in Christ and where He wants to take us for the rest of our days on this earth. Enjoy reading on.

In Him,

Nikki

Acknowledgements

Thank you Jesus for your amazing love and for bleeding forgiveness for me!

Thank you to my husband and son for your love throughout the comings and goings of this life.

Thank you to my family for support through the challenges I faced.

Thank you to my friends for your excitement and support.

Chapter 1

Choices

Ultimately there are two choices in each decision. You have the option of choosing the right or wrong one. You won't always make the right choices each time, but you have the ability to. The outcome of the choice you may not know, but making decisions and taking responsibility for them go hand in hand. It is so easy to blame someone else, especially your parents, but it's not right. Your parents did the best they knew how from the way they were raised. This is regarding the normal, dysfunctional families, not the abusive. There are many types of abuse and a great deal of pain comes from them all. I suggest you seek professional/Christian counseling so that you may become healthy and help the generational curse to stop at you. Think about forgiving the things in your past and yourself. This will take the guilt from you and a major weight will be lifted off your shoulders.

I have tried to blame my parents for the way they dealt with me throughout my life, but they wouldn't carry my poor choices. Now that I am older I realize they shouldn't have to. It is not their fault that I had a bad self esteem and strived to be popular, unfortunately starting a sexual pattern at the young age of 14. I could have taken my mom's advice from her experience, about not giving myself away, but I had to try it out for myself. I would try anything and date anybody who showed me attention. I thought it made me somebody. Nothing could happen to me. I was just having fun. I was doing what felt good to me. I was living life to the fullest; so I thought.

As I was growing up, I knew it all. I did not need anyone to tell me what I could and couldn't do. I could take care of myself. What an attitude for someone who never experienced the world. I spent a lot of my childhood being deceitful and playing my parents against one another, to get my own way. Pleasing me and, of course, the guy I was with is what I cared most about. Well, something did happen to me. I got pregnant at 19. I was dating two guys at the time, a waitress, and a student. What was I going to do? You think that's not so bad. OK, let's say I was also a drinker, druggy, and struggled with bulimia. I was in no shape to be a mom. The guy will be supportive right? This was a scary question for me being that I was sleeping with two guys. I decided shamefully to tell both of them. One said, "Have a good life" and the other was disappointed, but cared about me enough to stick around. Every guy and every situation is different. You will never know how they will react. After much thought I decided I was not able to care for this child on my own so I would be a birth mom. This meant placing my baby for adoption. Adoption is an extremely loving choice when you are unable to meet your child's needs. I did have faith in God when I was younger and knew that having an abortion was taking a life and it was wrong. "This day I call heaven and earth as witnesses against you that I have set before you life and death, blessings and curses. Now choose life, so that you and your children may live and that you may love the Lord your God, listen to his voice and hold fast to him" (Deuteronomy 30:19-20a).

Abortion has so many negative consequences. Yes you don't have the responsibility, but PAS – Post Abortion Syndrome is real. "The symptoms of it are guilt, anxiety, avoidance behaviors, psychological numbing, and depression."

I was never able to choose a family for my baby because when I was two and a half months pregnant I had a miscarriage. I remember that painful morning like it was yesterday. After this happened I had a DNC (dilation and curettage) which was explained to me as the scraping of my cervix to remove anything that wasn't excreted with the miscarriage. I just thought that if you got pregnant you had the baby or placed the baby for adoption. I never thought I could actually lose my baby. I did not grieve the loss of my baby, so I struggled for a long time with it.

The one thing I did realize was that I needed to get my life right with God. My parents had become adamant prayer warriors by now and they were hoping I would return to what was right—believing in and following God. They knew that I was headed for destruction if my life did not change. I had no direction, no solid plan for my life. I needed to turn my life over to God and stop being selfish. "For I know the plans I have for you," declares the Lord, "plans to prosper you and not to harm you, plans to give you a hope and a future. Then you will call upon me and come and pray to me, and I will listen to you. You will seek me and find me when you seek me with all your heart" (Jeremiah 29:11-13).

Remember choices are like grocery shopping. No matter what items you put in your cart you have to pay for them. Whether you pay cash now or credit later you must pay. Whether the consequences of your choices happen now or later, they will be there. So as you grow up and make decisions, what choices will you make that may affect the rest of your life?

I found that filling my mind with encouraging thoughts helped me make some better decisions. Some ideas are reading the Bible, listening to Christian music, and getting connected to a local youth group.

Please listen! It's time to take responsibility for your actions and accept the consequences. Put your childhood behind, put your past behind and look ahead with me.

Your life is depending on it

Chapter 2

The Perfect Shape

A Pastor once told me the heart has a mold inside made just for Jesus and until we accept Him into our hearts, we can try everything else, but **no thing** will fill the void. This chapter will show you the choices I made to try to fill my void.

I tried to fill up my void experimenting with sex, drugs, and alcohol. The more I did, the deeper the void in my heart. I chose all these things which hardened my heart and, therefore, determined my attitude in my adolescent years. I wanted so badly to be liked by guys that I risked what I believed and knew to be the truth for pleasure. I felt I needed their approval so I would give myself sexually and get a broken heart in return. The sad thing is, I thought this is all I had to offer. This is such a lie to young women from the devil. I learned that a guy stays a little longer when they don't get what they want because they like a chase. I also learned if they don't stick around it is their loss; don't beat yourself up over it. He may date the girl who is willing to be aggressive, but that is not the type of girl he would want to bring home to meet his family. Don't freely give away what God intended to be given once.

After I got pregnant, I started to reevaluate the way I lived my life, always pleasing people. I wanted to change. I realized this wasn't the best way because trying to impress people was clouding the person God intended me to be. By the way, I figured this out a little too late. My parents were fed up with my disobedient attitude, so they kicked me out of the house. Quite frankly I thought it was a joke, finally putting their foot down, but after I realized the joke was on me, I knew how much my parents really loved me. They only wanted the best for my life.

I moved back home after a couple of months and became involved with the youth group at the church my parents attended. I was then asked to be the kindergarten teacher at the affiliated Christian school and I accepted. I was involved with so many teens and young children, so I stopped doing drugs and drinking and started reading my Bible and running. I wanted to set an example in my church and school.

My first year of teaching was great. I was finishing my two year degree at a local community college. I also became accountable to students and teachers alike. My second year of teaching I realized I wanted to go back to college and move with my parents to Syracuse, New York. I was accepted to LeMoyne College in Syracuse, where my father was an alumnus, and was excited to start a new chapter in my life. In the meantime I had traveled to South Carolina to see a guy I had gone on a couple of dates with. This was the first guy I had not been sexually active with.

When I saw him the thought occurred to me, "no one will know if I have sex with him this one time; who would it hurt?" I forgot I would be hurting myself and my family. I also would be disappointing all the kids and teens that looked up to me. That one thought became a choice and changed my life. How could I be in the same position again? If only I had let God change my heart earlier I may not have made that choice.

My heart was extremely burdened by my future and this crisis pregnancy. I needed an emotional heart transplant and it needed to happen right away or the same thing would keep happening. There were a few steps I had to take if I didn't want my life to keep ending up in the same place.

I had to repent of my sins and ask the Lord for forgiveness, call my parents and tell them, being I would be living with them, and tell the father, Gerrod. Abortion did cross my mind, because I was so scared and ashamed, but the thought didn't last long.

"Above all else, guard your heart, for it is the wellspring of life" (Proverbs 4:43). *Wellspring* means fountain or source. You do have to guard your heart because what gets in there can easily become your destination.

Your life is depending on it

Chapter 3

Think About It

As young women we don't think, "I am looking so forward to being taken advantage of tonight, and I hope he breaks my heart so I can sit in my room and eat ice cream and cry for a week." No this sounds so foolish. The way I thought about myself portrayed this attitude and yours may too. Guys can sense the girl with the lowest self-esteem, the one who either keeps her head down acting shy, or the one who pretends to be the life of the party, just searching for attention. They know who we are. Think about it!

Next time you go out on a date or to a party don't dress to get the guy or to be noticed. Dress with confidence in yourself. If you have to be worried about your cleavage or how your butt looks in the jeans you painted on, you probably shouldn't be wearing them. Think about it!

I remember wanting to draw attention to myself and wanting to be noticed. The only way I knew how to do this was wear clothes that were revealing. I did this very thing when I went to see Gerrod. It obviously worked because he invited me back to his room. One thing led to another, it all happened so fast. I didn't even ask if he had protection. This is plain foolish and crazy. These days you are risking your own well being, and if you get pregnant, your baby's well being. This is just so you feel wanted. Think about it!

Maybe you do like the guy you are with now and you say, but he loves me and it feels right. Just remember babies are real. STD's are real. AIDS is real. Let's face it, if you can lie down so easily—protection or not—it can happen to you. Let's not be naïve to the fact that anything can happen to you if you are not careful. **Careful is being abstinent.** Think about it!

Why is it that mouthing back to our parents (family) and saying "NO" to their rules and suggestions is so easy, but saying "NO" to sex is just too hard. We think; "What will my friends think of me? Will he make fun of me? I don't want him to break up with me." Who cares what they think; how do you feel? Will they be the ones taking care of you or your baby if something were to happen and you needed help? No one ever thinks like that...

Yes, the very first passionate night with Gerrod became the first day of a new life growing inside me. It was also the beginning of nine months of pressure and stress I wasn't ready for.

I got down on my knees and really cried out to God. I asked for forgiveness and repented of the way I had lived my life for the past years and for my more recent actions. I don't think I ever cried so much. It felt so good to get right with God. I also prayed for strength to let my parents and Gerrod know. The thoughts going through my mind getting ready to tell my parents again were heartbreaking. I picked up the phone with my shaking hands, dialed holding my breath and then heard my mother's voice. I told her the scenario through many tears and she said in a saddened voice, "pack your bags and come to Syracuse now. We can deal with it when you get here." I was relieved. I knew she was disappointed, but there was opportunity to talk about it. I knew I would have to face my father and what would he think about his baby girl pregnant again? Just thinking of it made me hurt. My sister also lived in Syracuse, so I knew she would be a shoulder to lean on when I got there.

The next call was to Gerrod. I was shaky and anxious, but I knew I had to do it. I was terrified of rejection. He had his life down south. He had his own business and traveled a lot. We weren't even dating; what would happen? His life was fancy cars, expensive clothes and flashy women. We cared for each other, but our lives were so different. I knew his thoughts weren't to settle down and I didn't want that right now either. I had to prepare myself for what he would say. The conversation wasn't great. He was extremely angry. I was extremely emotional. We left the conversation that he would tell his mother and family and I would move to Syracuse, for support when the school year ended. This was the only plan that was made between us. I was frightened to tell the teachers at school. I didn't want people to talk bad about me.

About three weeks later I still hadn't heard from him and my heart was aching. What were we going to do? Would I place the baby with a loving couple or would I raise him on my own, sharing custody? What would I do for a job; I only had a two-year degree?

The next couple months were filled with questions until I found a crisis pregnancy center, New Hope Family Services, which encouraged me in my decision making. I had drawn closer to the Lord in this time because I felt I was being pulled in so many directions by my family. Everyone had an opinion while trying to be helpful. It was frustrating. The counselor I had just encouraged me enough to make a plan to parent and also to look at waiting family portfolios. Gerrod wasn't sure what to do or how he felt, still. He was confused and had issues of his own he was dealing with. Even though we didn't talk much I prayed for him nightly. I prayed that he would do God's will and I prayed the Lord would soften his hard heart and bring him to his knees.

The wonderful thing was that I had his mother's support whatever the decision because she had been through both. She placed her daughter 33 years ago with a loving family and then four years later she was pregnant, divorced and a single mom. She was very supportive and would talk to Gerrod about taking responsibility for the future of this child.

I was seven months pregnant when the Lord spoke to me one Sunday morning and gave me my answer through a sermon that was preached. The overall message was to keep the baby. I was grateful for the message because I would be looking at families for the baby that Tuesday, being that I only had two months until show time. It was a confirmation when both my parents told me they felt the same way. By this time I had gained 50 lbs. and was becoming self-conscious. I also started getting a little uptight thinking of all the things I would need and thinking of the many plans and arrangements I would have to make for the new arrival.

Gerrod and I talked more often as the time was getting closer. I was eight and a half months pregnant when he decided to visit Syracuse. It was hard for me to see him the way I was and he couldn't believe it was I. I obviously looked different that passionate night eight and a half months prior. We made some plans, talked about names, and talked a little about his long term goals.

At this time I was trying to hold on to his every word because I thought there may be a chance for us to be together, even though he said he was never selling his business and never moving to Syracuse. He started to show some support for me and I showed much support for him and his business. The church family, that my parents were members of, showed me so much love and they were a big support system for the baby, both Gerrod and me and our future. It was neat to see God's Amazing love over the next two years.

Once again, I found that filling my mind with godly thoughts and words was helpful to me. "Do not be anxious about anything, but in everything, by prayer and petition, with thanksgiving, present your requests to God. And the peace of God, which transcends all understanding will guard your hearts and your minds in Christ Jesus" (Philippians 4:6-7).

Your life is depending on it

Chapter 4

A Special Package

Let's think for a minute about the person you love and where he lives. Now think how you would feel if you just found out that someone totally destroyed the outside and ransacked the inside of his home. I am more than positive you would feel angry and hurt that someone would do this to your loved one's property. I believe that God feels the same way when we put our bodies down and let guys take advantage of them, defacing the very temple he made for Himself to dwell.

My beautiful son, Colin Phoenix Speer was born February 14, 2002 at 6:56 PM weighing 9lbs., 6oz., and was 20 inches long. Having a baby not only changes your heart and mind it changes your body, big time! Now I had to lose the 60 lbs. I had gained. I tried not to make it my ultimate focus. My focus now was the little boy that God blessed me with and I started realizing the Amazing Love God has for us.

Gerrod put most of his business off and stayed for a couple of weeks with my family and me. He was a big help and a great daddy. Spending each day with him and seeing him with Colin, I started falling in love with him.

I soon started throwing myself at him whenever he showed interest in me. I noticed that he didn't really want to be intimate with me and I felt completely insecure when this happened. I always thought that if a guy gave me a compliment or did something nice to or for me, I had to give something back—myself.

When he went back to work down south I would call him each night. I was reaching out to him and not holding my ground on what God wanted for my life. See, he didn't need me throwing myself at him, nor did he want that. We were in an awkward position as it was, not knowing each other well with a child; he didn't want it to happen again. He didn't think it was very attractive that the mother of his baby was throwing herself at him. He could get that anywhere. He thought I had more to offer than just my body, being that I kept professing I was a Christian. I sure wasn't acting like one.

Most men don't want a girl who is willing to do anything. They want a girl with confidence in herself. Heed the warning; if you give your body freely you will be taken advantage of.

Gerrod would try to come home every two to three weeks for one week at a time. I began to get extremely angry with him when he wouldn't have sex with me. I wanted him to need me. I was trying to do God's will in the meantime, but I was not following His plan acting this way. "Flee from sexual immorality. All other sins a man commits are outside his body, but he who sins sexually sins against his own body… you were bought with a price. Therefore honor God with your body" (1Corinthians 6:18& 20).

I decided to stop being stubborn and get back on track once again. I began to pray for Gerrod each night, as a father and a friend and I also asked God for help with my self-control. This started to form a great friendship between us and when he came home we talked about both of our life goals and things we wanted for Colin. We felt the same about a lot of things except the fact that I always mentioned Jesus. Quite frankly he thought I was a little overboard about the whole thing. Nevertheless he started to respect me more.

I couldn't do this all on my own. I really did need help. I began praying more and giving myself less to Gerrod. There were many nights I would cry myself to sleep because I was living with my parents, working part time, staying up late, and making arrangements on my own. This was incredibly tiring. I am truly grateful to my parents and sister for their help when it came to babysitting and giving me some time for myself.

All in all, Gerrod started changing. He would call every now and then to say he not only missed Colin, but me too. He was mentioning how tired of the business, stress, and traveling he was. This touched my heart because I saw God changing him.

I had no idea that the people in his business were becoming unethical and immoral and he was so mentally tired. He wanted to be closer to us. Slowly things were changing and God was working it out, not only for Colin and me, but for His Glory.

My body was now changing slowly and getting back to normal along with the heart change God was doing in me. I was seeing how less can become more, how stepping back and giving God a chance to work was a great idea.

Sometimes when we don't listen or learn the first, second, or third time, similar circumstances come around to challenge us again seeking a new and different response. They shape us into the special package that God intended us to be.

Sometimes we need big boulders in the road, to help us stop and think. Please don't wait until you smash into the boulder three or four times. Take notice now of what God is trying to show you. He wants the best for you. His best is not always our plan, but it is what we need...

Your life is depending on it

Chapter 5

Worth More Than A Diamond

God did a great deal of changing when it came to Gerrod. He opened his eyes to a whole new world. That whole new world was cold, snowy Syracuse, New York. He was moving from beautiful, sunny Charleston, South Carolina. Yes, Gerrod was my answered prayer. The Lord not only brought him back to Syracuse, He changed his heart. After moving here and a couple of months at his new job as a car salesman, he accepted Jesus as his savior. He no longer wanted to live his life for himself. He didn't want to carry the weight on his shoulders from his past lifestyle. It was a bittersweet time to have him with us.

He found an apartment so that he could have some quality time with his little boy. Gerrod and I also started going on dates, something we did little of before, to get to know each other. We had so much fun together. We also started attending a church together and met a Christian couple that had experienced similar circumstances and helped us tremendously.

I was getting weary of the situation, I wanted a commitment. I wanted God to hurry up. I was getting in the way again.

> "Show me your ways, O LORD, teach me your paths; guide me in your truth and teach me, for you are God my Savior, and my hope is in you all day long. Remember, O LORD, your great mercy and love, for they are from old. Remember not my sins of my youth and my rebellious ways; according to your love remember me, for you are good, O LORD. Good and upright is the LORD; therefore he instructs sinners in his ways. He guides the humble in what is right and teaches them his way"
>
> —Psalm 25:4-9

Through this time God was trying to show me to be patient and grateful. I had to remember, He brought Gerrod this far to make the situation work out for His glory, not mine. His ways are far greater than what we could imagine. I had no idea the way the Lord was working in Gerrod's heart.

To my surprise he had gone to see my dad and asked for my hand and then at midnight January 2004 he decided to ask me to be his better half for the rest of our lives. It seemed like a dream come true. I said "yes." We were married in Las Vegas, Nevada one month later. Our families were praying for this to happen and they were very excited. And now you think we lived happily ever after. I am afraid that life is not like the storybook endings we know. In our first year of marriage we experienced a great deal of loss, pain, and humbling. Gerrod's cousin at the young age of 21 passed away suddenly in April; Gerrod struggled with many health problems; Gerrod joined a partnership; we bought a home in August; Gerrod split with his partner that left him with no job in October; his mother became extremely ill the same week, leaving Colin and me alone for 3 months. It was a challenging first year, yet a year that taught us a lot about ourselves and brought us closer to the Lord.

This is when I decided to volunteer my time at New Hope Family Services to give back to the place that brought me much hope when I was in my crisis pregnancy. I felt the Lord brought me through this circumstance to share with other young women.

Gerrod moving home, being proposed to, getting married and buying a home could never compare to the path that both Gerrod and I chose. This decision to follow the Lord and raise our son the way He would want has changed our lives. We still have heartaches and we are not done growing and learning, but we are ready and willing to seek Him.

You may never know what your future holds, but you can change the path you're going down today. Remember sin brings chaos and pain and Jesus brings serenity and life in the midst of circumstances. Which will you choose?

Your life is depending on it

Chapter 6

The Narrow Road

In the first chapter I mentioned choices. Deciding what road to travel is the biggest one. I believe there are two roads, wide and narrow. Popular opinion states the wide road is fun and exciting and the narrow road is dull and boring. I believe this opinion is false. The following is how I would describe both paths.

The wide road looks so enticing. There is so much to do on this journey all alone. There are no boundaries, no rules; anything goes. You can do what ever pleases you. You can go wherever, date whomever, drink whatever and do drugs however. It's all good as long as it feels good. This seems more than thrilling for the traveler. It most certainly does because no human likes to be told what to do. This is because we are born with sin. We have a rebellious nature. Genesis 3 states how this all began. We just want to try things out for ourselves. We don't want to listen. We feel as though we will miss out on something if we don't. This road is hot, sandy, and dark. There are no signs, no boundaries. It leaves you thirsty for more. There is not much trust in people on this path because no one can be looked up to. There is a lot of sickness, bitterness, anger, wrath, and a plethora of heartache. Anything goes and after a while it is like a mouse on a spinning wheel; there is no end. People call this living life to the fullest.

The other road could be described as more of a hill, but, a well lit, firm-footed, narrow path with many people to come alongside of you, full of wisdom. There is no other deviation and there are many signs on the path to guide you along. There is also a fence as a boundary that you are unable to cross. These boundaries keep you from the sharks in the beautiful ocean that lines the path. Sometimes there are potholes in this road that you may fall in, but you are quickly pulled out if you yell for help. There are small benches and water fountains to be refreshed at. This is a serene, yet challenging path.

As young women we should not have to make extreme, adult decisions like having babies; we should be enjoying life with our families and friends. Here are some fun things to do on a date or with some friends: board games, bowling, rollerblading, walking, running, swimming, playing video games, going to the zoo, going out to dinner, cooking for a friend in need, doing yard work together, doing a fun project, making cookies together, planning and throwing a party together, taking a day trip, cleaning up the trash in a neighborhood, volunteering, investing in a neighbor's life and definitely getting involved with a youth group.

These are just some ideas to get you started. I am sure you could think of other things to do based on your personality. Have a good time with these ideas. Have fun and enjoy your teen years in a healthy way. Don't grow up too soon.

Choosing the road that everyone else is taking is not that much fun and definitely not free. Choosing the narrow road is free. You may pay with guilt, shame, an STD, or possibly DEATH! This doesn't sound so fun when you look at it like this. Everyone is looking for the right path and all the answers. My father wrote a poem in 1960 titled "Answers" He was only 18 at the time. I want to share this with you.

> Today we live in a world of temptation, fear and strife. The true meaning of joy and love is lost in daily life.
> The future seems so strange because we know not what's in store. Yet science seems to know the cause that makes us strive for more.
> They tell us we must reach the moon and be the first one's there. And maybe we will reach it soon, but the answers won't be there.
> The answers aren't in outer space they're not that far away. They're in that small and sacred place where you and I must pray!

Girls, no human being has all the answers. There are so many choices in life and each day you have a new opportunity to make a positive change. You are worth more than diamonds. You are beautiful and special. Take care of and cherish the one and only body God has given to his precious little girl. He also gave you a mind, heart, and soul to make good life decisions. "Trust the Lord with all your heart and lean not on your own understanding; in all your ways acknowledge Him, and He will make your paths straight" (Proverbs 3:5-6). Choose the road of life you will walk down. It could lead to Your Creator, Your Father, Your Friend...

Your life is depending on it

Chapter 7

Come As You Are

I share my story with you to let you know that God loved me enough to stop me and I was finally willing to listen. If you are reading this right now He loves you just as much. No I am not crazy. What would be crazy is if I never told you how I came to know God in a personal way and how my life choices changed because of it. "For God so loved the world that He gave His one and only Son, that whoever believes in Him shall not perish, but have eternal life" (John 3:16). This means accepting Jesus as your leader, friend, and father.

You think you are damaged goods and no one will want you; think again. Come as you are to Him, no matter if you are beaten, bruised, torn, shattered, used, or abused. Whatever you may be, He wants you in Heaven with Him and living a life for him here on earth.

By living for Him you will be free from parenting or placing your baby, guilt from the night before, and worry about a number of issues when you live for yourself. You will have a joy deep inside no matter what comes along. This joy will come by spending time with God and reading His word, the Bible each day.

God is a perfect gentleman. He will not make you do anything. He gave you the ability to choose what road to walk down. God gave you free will. He would never force His love on you. When you are forced to do something, you most likely regret it and back away. He wants you to get to know Him and this will only happen when you reach out to Him on your own. You are His child and he wants a relationship with you, but in order to do this you need to spend time with Him. Come as you are to the foot of the cross. He is waiting with open arms.

Girls, saying a simple prayer such as the one that follows, will show the Lord that you mean business. He will take up residence in your heart and I promise you, you will be changed.

> Dear God,
> I know I am a sinner and I want to turn from my old ways, but I need you to help me. Please come into my heart. Thank you for sending your son, Jesus to die on the cross for me so that I might be able to have a relationship with you and that my sins would be forgiven. Lord from this moment on I want to be more like you. I love you.

Remember you can't change the past; you don't know the future, but you can start new today. It's not too late. Come as you are and let the God of grace and mercy lead you on this journey of life and experience, His amazing love.

His life paid the price for it!

If this book has helped you in any way,
please write and share with me your story.

kitaspeer@yahoo.com

A Guy's Perspective

I thought hearing from Gerrod would help you understand how a guy may think when he hears such news as, "I'm pregnant." I asked him a few questions about his childhood, life and about the pregnancy. The following are the answers recorded on June 8th, 2005.

What are some dramatic things you experienced in your childhood?

I was brought up by my mom because my parents divorced when I was a baby. My father and I never had a strong relationship. He never spent time with me and thought that buying me gifts would make up for it.

I grew up thinking I was an only child, until age 11 when a cousin of mine had an unplanned pregnancy. This prompted my mom to tell me about my sister, Holly, who was placed for adoption in the 1970's. My mother signed and stated in legal documents that she would never look for her. This was a closed adoption. When I became the legal age of 18 I found my sister. We have had a close relationship for the last 11 years and have realized how much alike we are.

How did you feel the day I told you I was pregnant?

I felt betrayed, angry, trapped, and very apprehensive. I felt I always had the answers in business situations, but in this life circumstance the answer wasn't as clear.

How did you feel during the pregnancy?

I wasn't around for eight and a half months, because I felt if I wasn't there I wouldn't have to deal with the reality of being a dad. I wasn't sure I knew how or if I was ready.

What happened when Colin was born?

I couldn't be in the room because Nikki didn't want me there, but when I finally got to see him I knew this was where I wanted and needed to be. Colin gave my empty life meaning. Everyone kept saying how much he looked like me and it made me feel more like a daddy.

How was your heart changing?

When I went back to work down south I was surrounded by all the things I thought I wanted, but realized I was the loneliest I had ever been. God put it in my heart to come home and I realized it was the right thing. I found a job and an apartment and spent more time with Colin and Nikki. On December 17, 2003, I gave my heart to the Lord. It's been challenging and wonderful ever since.

What would you say to a guy/girl dealing with an unplanned pregnancy?

As I think back on the situation I wonder how I could have felt some of the ways I did, but we are human. We don't always have the answers. I would urge young people to trust in God because even at your worst God loves you and He sent his son Jesus to die for you. He won't let you down like some earthly fathers do.

No matter what your childhood, we all have the ability as young men and women to change. Make your decisions on what God would want for your life rather than selfish reasons. It will come back to you tenfold. God will bless you.

Prayer Journal

(Date your prayers and God's answers.
It's a good way to keep the faith.)

25 Things I Like About Myself

(This will help you realize you have a lot more to offer than your body.)

1. ______________________________
2. ______________________________
3. ______________________________
4. ______________________________
5. ______________________________
6. ______________________________
7. ______________________________
8. ______________________________
9. ______________________________
10. ______________________________
11. ______________________________
12. ______________________________

13. ____
14. ____
15. ____
16. ____
17. ____
18. ____
19. ____
20. ____
21. ____
22. ____
23. ____
24. ____
25. ____

Endnotes

1. Terri Reisser, M.S.,M.F.T., *Healing After Abortion*, Focus on the Family Literature, 2002, 5.

*All quotes taken from Life Application Study Bible, New International Version.

To order additional copies of

AMAZING *Love*

Have your credit card ready and call:

1-877-421-READ (7323)

or please visit our web site at
www.pleasantword.com

Also available at:
www.amazon.com
and
www.barnesandnoble.com

Printed in the United States
43417LVS00005B/58-66

9 781414 105727